THIS

BY MI(

BODY LANGUAGE 12

A MIDSUMMER NIGHT'S PRESS

New York

For Jason, who persisted

Cover painting © by Stefano Cipollari

A Midsummer Night's Press
16 West 36th Street
2nd Floor
New York, NY 10018
amidsummernightspress@gmail.com
www.amidsummernightspress.com

I am grateful to the editors of the publications where some of these poems previously appeared, sometimes in a different form or with different titles. *420pus:* "Buffy Rerun Poem"; *BLOOM:* "Pictography"; *Brooklyn Review* "Twilight in the City"; *Columbia Poetry Review:* "A Brief History," "Gladiators," "Imaginary Playmate," "Investiture" "Pictography," "Supermarionation"; *Court Green:* "Confession"; La Petite Zine: "After," "Instead of Names," "Investiture"; *Painted Bride Quarterly:* "Prologue"; roger: "The Old Meaning/Moaning Dichotomy"; *Softblow:* "Later than I Would Like It to Be"; *This New Breed: Gents, Bad Boys, and Barbarians 2* (edited by Rudy Kikel, Windstorm Creative): "Exotic", "Prologue"

Thanks to friends who have read and commented on these poems: Lauren Cardwell, Veronica Castrillón, Peter Covino, Jean Gallagher, Patricia Spears Jones, Jennifer L. Knox, Ada Limón, Daniel Nester, Barbara Ravage, Hilary Sideris, and Marion Curtis Wrenn.

Thanks to teachers, both of old: Phyllis Cohen, Vera Fried, Anita Malta, and the late Judy Slater; and of late: Elizabeth Alexander, Stephen Dunn, Edward Hirsch, Marie Howe, Phillis Levin, Philip Levine, Sharon Olds, Marie Ponsot, Robert Polito, Martha Rhodes, Tom Sleigh, and Jean Valentine. Thanks to the administrators and staff of the Creative Writing Program at New York University from 2003-2005: Allison Brotherton, Russell Carmony, Melissa Hammerle, and Danielle Nigro-Bullock. Thanks to my editor and publisher, Lawrence Schimel, and to Julie R. Enszer, who played *shadchan*.

Designed by Aresográfico www.diegoareso.com

First edition, March 2014.

ISBN-13: 978-1-938334-08-5

Prited in Spain.

CONTENTS

This Life Now

My First Ten Plague Years

What liberty a loosened spirit brings!
—Emily Dickinson

VARIATIONS

A few words go a long way between us;
as they must, since not much time
remains for more than this.

I saw you standing on the fire escape,
arms spread wide to catch the setting sun,
head tossed back, shoulders
flirting with the shadows,

as if you could elude the waning day,
or *time* and *again* could become one,
or time could stand still between lovers,
not knowing what tomorrow brings,

nor caring where yesterday we walked,
like phrases, not quite nonsense,
but with a logic and connection
not at all designed until they meet

in composition, improvised, like a blues—
no melody planned, but only trusting
our sense of intervals.

PROLOGUE

When I think of how it began,
I enter an endless regression—

before the visit to the counselor's office,
blood draw, awful flu in May,

before I let Tony fuck me raw to say I was sorry.
But that wasn't the first time.

The first time I got fucked was in 1984.
We already knew what was risky—

I took his cum anyway.
They barely had a virus yet, so

I chose to believe it was something else:
poppers or multiple partners—

some cofactor of a gayness I was too
ingénue to have indulged.

I deserved to have one time skin to skin,

at least the first one,
at least that.

TONY POEM

By the time we meet, Bobby is dead and the guitar
lies untouched in its dusty case in a corner of the "dungeon,"

the dark hole you sleep in beneath your parents' house.

You keep drinking and fucking,
ultimate bad-boy fuck machine,

vodka-fueled rock-n-roll Quasimodo.

Weekends, diligent, you mop the floor of your
mother's beauty parlor,

just the right dilution of bleach and soapy water.

You leave me in the middle of the night,
hang out on the boardwalk with junkies and hustlers,

they rip you off when you fall asleep on a bench.

While I'm at work you write things on my computer
that will haunt me
when you're gone.

Every revision omits more—
          who infected whom, what you knew and when.

What remains—

          Some cassettes you made for me,
     notebooks, clippings.

Photos of you onstage with your bass,
          hair plastered to your forehead,

open shirt a drenched banner

proclaiming you.

INSTEAD OF NAMES

Now I wait in familiar locations—
the park, the promenade,
any place I think you might find me.

When you arrive, I sidle up—
no words offered by way of introduction,
just a lie I tell with my eyes,
to grant permission or deny it,
to hide my shame at being self-absorbed,
cobbled together of disparate parts—
posture, hair and nails, clothing.

For a while you stay and I think it's what I wanted—
to kneel before you beneath the trees,
beside the dark river, under icy stars.

I SEE YOU OFTEN
AROUND THE CITY

Once I saw you walking down Eighth Avenue,
long frame, Aztec face, searing grin—

I thought you were talking to no one, excitedly,
which would be like you, but in fact it was

a hands-free cell phone. Today I saw you
cross-legged on the retaining wall

in Central Park, shorn of your long thick tresses,
writing in your diary—

something about Anaïs, or how you crawled
into bed with your mother's lovers

                                        while she
made *flautas* in the kitchen.

When I see you now, you are just as you were before
(neither dead, nor missing, nor unaccounted for).

AFTER

You come late.
The others have gone
and left me here
expecting no one.
I wasn't waiting for you.
The waiting is over,
but leaving isn't easy.

It must look strange to you,
this world
of darkened corners,
hands and knees.
It only gets colder
after midnight.
The crackheads never go home.

How young you are—
I smell it on your hair,
feel it in the flush of your skin.
I wanted you only
for the usual cut and run;
but now that you're here,
I don't want you to go.

See where you have come—
this is a different time;
this is after.
A few of us remain,
but nobody knows
if we are survivors
or merely hangers on.

You still have time—
there's no glory here
and some say no love,
where bodies are counted
and sheets are burned.
Go back the way you came.
Go home and sleep.

DAYS OF 1999

Summer strangles like a telephone cord—
    I must remember to call if a day goes by,
to say I'm sorry for wrongs I have not done

    so as to court you.
Smooth, brown, easily wounded,
    you roll onto your stomach when it's time.

Silently I invoke the ghost of
    He-Who-Fucked-Like-an-Animal;
behind your back I make preparations

    and send you over the edge.
Ah, *cariño*, you remind me
    when love was measured in transgressions—

committed, imagined, regretted.
    Then too it was summer,
sorrow thick and wet,

like breathing through a hot towel.
That summer is gone,
    dried and crumbled like seaweed.

I smell the salt on your hair sometimes.
    You bring me the sea and all its ghosts,
the rale of breakers on the sand.

TWILIGHT IN THE CITY

Car horns blow in on breezes,
fill the spaces left by fading light.

Color drains from this room,
time floats in space where once
there was a microwave oven.

All that's left here—
the party we threw, P.J.'s dance tapes,
that boy who wanted to sleep with you
and kept asking when I was going home.

ANOTHER TONY POEM

But tonight, if I went down
under the boardwalk, would I find you there,
leaning against a pillar or a chain-link fence,
like when you were 13, getting your
grown-up size cock sucked by a hungry boy?
Nope. Next to your grandparents, maybe;
and I wonder what it looks like,
what your stone says after name and dates—
Lived in fear? Died of complications?
Remember the dumpster we passed that time,
those people living behind it, and I said
That's what I'm afraid of, that you'll end up that way.
"How can you compare," you demanded
in the Stoli-and-Marlboro-soaked rasp
that made me quiver; and maybe you were right:
People like that go on for years and years,
living aloof from us who pass and stare.
It was never your lot to linger that way:
You burned, then exploded, then were gone.

WORDS AND THINGS

Near the end we walked along the beach;
        you said we felt disconnected,
    like a sentence with no conjunctions.

Once we had shared—
        razors, toothbrush, a blanket,
    like sea and air share the horizon,

    reflecting, penetrating each other,
each better suited to any given thing,

    like air to birds, sea to fish,
yet both hospitable to rainstorms,

    and each with something unique
to offer sunsets.

Near the end we talked about words,
    how actions speak louder
    but are generally inadequate

        to hypotheses
           and other logical or affective relations

whose truth or validity
　　　　　are only apparent over time

　　as in

The pen is mightier than the sword
　　　　　　　　　　　　or the phrase
　　Killing with kindness.

ANOTHER TONY POEM

I'm glad there was a moment in my life
when I was foolish enough to love the likes of you.

Portrait of the Artist as a Young Sodomite

—

When you wet the bed first
it is warm then it gets cold.
— James Joyce

A BRIEF HISTORY

In 1960, by my mother, my father's bread is buttered
    without irony.
Then, the word "luncheonette" was uttered without irony.

Sodium lamps surround our housing project like a stalag.
Home alone, watching *Rosemary's Baby*, I shuddered
    without irony.

High school girls wonder why Michael won't date them.
In a pizzeria, over a vial of pills, her eyelashes fluttered,
    without irony.

In the lower bunk I ask permission before removing my briefs.
From above, "I love you," stuttered without irony.

SUPERMARIONATION

In our bedroom chop shop
     my big brother and I
scoured through NASCAR colorful cardboard boxes,

reliquaries of polyurethane remnants,
     spare tires and hub caps,
demolished chassis and bodies stripped from last year's
         car models,

from which we'd effect a new kind of carburetion,

combining internal-combustion castoffs
     into space-age cruisers and jet-propelled craft,

Supercars for our Captain Scarlets of the mind.

IMAGINARY PLAYMATE

My parents questioned me, suspecting you existed.
I affirmed you in a general way,
but kept the intimate details to myself—

How clad in black trunks, but otherwise bare,
you rescued me from some always vague danger,

swept me from the ledge of a high building,
cradled me trembling in the crook of your arms,
and flew away with me—

My hand resting on the curve of your chest,
my hot tears falling on your pink nipple.

GLADIATORS

Kirk Douglas on the small black-and-white screen
    in the bedroom I share with my brother.

Spartacus arrives in chains at the gladiatorial school.

The trainer puts him in the center of the circle
    (loin cloth, bare chest).

Using brightly colored paints from wooden buckets
    he marks on Spartacus' torso
the location of blows that will kill a man with maximum
    efficiency.

Also in this film, or maybe it's another film, another
    Sunday afternoon, maybe *Ben-Hur*, it's all one
    film really, one black-and-white TV, one bedroom,
    one brother,

I watch galley-slaves, bare-backed, muscular, sweating,
    long dirty hair, unkempt beards,

and the slave driver's whip comes down on a bench,
    beats a rhythm for the slaves to row,

and some of them flag at their rowing and then the whip
      comes down on their backs—

bruises, streaks of blood,

sometimes buckets of water poured over their steaming
      heads or thrown in their parched faces, and
      sometimes a slave falls over

exhausted uncared for just dragged aside and replaced by
      another and I watch, ashamed, and I go into hiding.

MOD SQUAD

I didn't leave home, I was kicked out, Pete says to Linc as they drive conversing in close-ups through the night.

I had the hots for Pete, and for Wally Cleaver, and for Chip, the middle of Fred MacMurray's three sons, but never for any of the Brady boys, although possibly for the original youngest son (Chris) on *The Partridge Family,* the dark haired one with the big brown eyes (Jeremy Gelbwaks), not that blond dork (Brian Forster) who replaced him in season two.

Yes, Jeremy Gelbwaks was prepubescent, but so was I, so there was nothing icky about it.

A little later I had the hots for Doug Abrams, but that was real life, not TV.

Doug had light brown flyaway hair, the kind of hair boys would flick out of their eyes with a jerk of their neck in kind of a girlish way, and soft pink lips and the slightest bit of an overbite, and he was troublemaker enough to be bad boy sexy, but not so much as to trigger my withering sense of right and wrong.

Except that to have the hots for him was wrong; but that's a different story, and we were pubescent by then.

DIRECTIONAL

If I part my hair on the same side repeatedly,
I develop a cowlick (also called a spit curl),
so I vary the part periodically, sometimes
right, sometimes left. I wonder if I'm

misunderstood, if anyone thinks my action
signifies something. Because these things
do have meaning sometimes, like in the
seventies, when an earring on the right

meant a man was gay. Now, the origins of
this sign are obscure, but there's likely a
connection to codes developed in the sixties
in the S&M community, where (even today)

a colored hanky in the right rear pocket
marks the passive partner of a given
fetish (red for fisting, for example, or
yellow for piss), while a hanky on the left
means active.

Active and passive are to some extent
euphemisms for insertive and receptive, a

dichotomy also referred to as top and bottom. Later the code signaled top/bottom

roles for all gay sex, not just S&M, and various accessories flagged the distinction: a belt-clip key ring, a chain slipped over the epaulette of a leather jacket. Extending the

code from a sign for top/bottom to one for gay/straight suggests that top equates to masculine and is akin to straight, while bottom equates to feminine and is akin to

gay. Some might find this offensive. These days, men straight and gay wear earrings in both ears. It was a bigger deal when Joe Errante, on whom I had an aching high

school crush, got his ear pierced. I leaned in close to check out his new stud. Joe said, "Don't worry, it's on the left."

PICTOGRAPHY

They declared war on me,
but I was no warrior, so I left—
wandered deserts alone,
spoke no one's language,
knew no one's customs.
I invented civilization with every step—
every footprint a cuneiform wedge—
alphabet, syllabary, pictograph:
hope, love.

To escape detection,
I disguised myself as a human being,
wore clothing and parted my hair on the side,
ate animal and vegetable products,
lived among the natives,
pretending I was one of them.

I became the cinema clown
who mirrors his rival's every move,
retreats behind the doorway
or the column or the potted plant,
just as his opponent peeks around the corner.

INVESTITURE

Walking along Surf Avenue I see the Berlin night
scurry from the headlight of a Citroën.

When I turn the next corner,
Batman casts a shadow over moonlit Gotham,
and climbing down the stairs
to the cool sand beneath the boardwalk,
I am Orpheus descending,

down on my knees before you can say blow me.

Here in the dark I slake my thirst
for lies that taste like truth.

Here in the dark, the Heliconian Muses
thrust the vatic staff down my throat
and I assume my poetic mantle.

You press me against the piling—

I come in my jeans.
I come close to love.

OMMATIDIA

What about a good old-fashioned
ich-du type poem, like the old days,

Budweisers and brown paper bags,
high-school sweethearts

and gym-class heartthrobs,
the bad skin, bad teeth,

never saying, always doing,
the art of the locker room

drive-by, quick while the shower's
running, re-runs of *The Walton's*

and *The Twilight Zone.*
I had a friend who predicted John

would be the first Beatle to die,
but we were no longer speaking

by the time it came true,
by the time I'd gone

where I didn't belong,
the old hand trouble again,

many more where that came from,
names known and unknown,

loosening of the belt,
lowering of the zipper,

come into my parlor,
you're the spider, I'm the fly,

stand there many-refracted
in my compound eye.

SECRET

Remember when walks on the beach
led to trysts in the cool sand beneath the boardwalk?

Disease then crept through your body,
but you kept it at bay with a churning engine of desire.

Now you wash the virus away
like silt through a hollow drainpipe,

and this life now is the better life, but oh,
how the cool sand calls.

This Life Now

———

I don't want to sleep; I just want to be alive with you.
    —Lee Broder
      Methodist Hospital, Brooklyn. May 6, 2005

RANDOM

This fabric, once torn, cannot be mended.

You call it industrial chic; I call it
what I grew up with.

Our love has no trajectory.

We are a fait accompli, pen to paper,
shattering of silence.

THE REMEMBERED ONE

The good die young, but sometimes
      they come back, dripping with something
            we can't name or identify,
an acrid perfume, or they reach for us
            like a taproot, draining
our sweet wells of oblivion
            until we lie drenched in a common sweat,
            our bed sheet their burial shroud, their
      moldering crust.

I dreamt of Marcos last night.
      I thought he came to be buried,
            to be done with; but no, that caramel devil,
leaving his tangerine swim trunks wet on the floor,
            toweling his gorgon hair as he sits in my lap,
numbing me with the poppies
            of his opiate grin and reasserting his claim:

Why should *you* get the house,
      the husband, the PhD, while I chew on dirt
            and feed succeeding generations
of night crawlers?
            I can crawl the night too, you know, the

night is crawling
with me, with mine, with ours—
            us—
            while you pretend to walk, awake, alive.

Come with me, why don't you, make once and for all
        the descent you practiced so ably for so many years.
            I know a place with many darkened corners
where you can crawl on hands and knees
        like in the old days—
What's that you called it? *"the old ich-du..."*

We are beautiful there, and legion.
        We will keep you busy for centuries.
            And think what precious memories *he* will have,
here above—

This is the song you have waited so long to sing, isn't it?

EXOTIC

The delivery boy from the 24-hour diner
brings me a bleu cheeseburger deluxe, medium rare.
I seduce him at my apartment door.
His promise: "I fuck you every day."

Lebanese accent thick, sexy, slightly comic.
He waits for the elevator, straightens his apron,
never uses the future tense.
Sometimes I see him on the corner about noon,

just before he goes on shift,
leaning against the side of a building,
brown skin of his high cheekbones
tilted toward the sun.

Sometimes we greet each other,
sometimes his eyes are closed.

CASES

Nominative, locus of being;
the river rises, the river falls.

The genitive's whole, that of which one is part,
as the river's breath that sweetens us.

To the dative we abject ourselves,
as to the river we bring what we love.

Accusative: what we inflict upon another
as we enter the river.

Ablative—case of separation or, paradoxically,
        accompaniment:
We emerge from the river whole.

Where is the locative (vestigial in extant languages)?
Where our children wait patiently in the river?

By means of the instrumental we achieve our end:
With the river we enter eternity.

Vocative, whom we supplicate or implore:
River; oh, River; you, River!

THE OLD MEANING/MOANING
DICHOTOMY

On bad days I seek a theoretical basis
      for my actions, a point of origin, a strategy,
         a thread to pull me through,
         family tree, concentric circles,

dates of birth and death, lists. Because
      meaning is not so much in things
         as in the story the thing implies,
         like melody implies harmony,

a setting that makes the pattern perceptible,
      lets the tune make sense. Because
         being challenged is not the same as being
thwarted,
         and the progression from classical

to whatever comes after classical
      has to do with sympathy—familiarity with
         and fundamental acceptance of
         the implied organizing structure—

making departures from an implied standard
     without rejecting the standard outright.
          Our overriding impulse is toward
     resolution—
          this subsumes both the pleasure principle

and the death wish—coming and going.
     When we behave radically, or irrationally,
          it is because we do not perceive ourselves
               in meaningful relation to the field

and this is very distressing, even terrifying.
     This is chaos—the inability to perceive
          the ordering principle at work. And so I say
               on bad days I seek a theoretical basis

for my actions, or else I seek experience,
     drink experience, as if by sucking and swallowing
          I could replenish some heart center,
          something I did not even know was empty.

LATER THAN I WOULD
LIKE IT TO BE

Shadows lengthen on the cold pavement,
October stains the leaves on dry, rustling trees,
you become loam in the ground—
dissolve, disintegrate,
like words that made no difference on first hearing—

Words like:
Nobody has the flu for nine weeks;
see another doctor;
drinking will kill you before the virus has a chance.

Words like:
You do not have to die;
I love you;
I love you anyway.

Words like:

It's okay, it's okay.

CIVIL UNION

When I die, you say, you can take
hot young Russian boys home
and have sex with them in our bed;
but you must tell them about me.

Here I should capture you
in a deft array of telling details
that bring you to life in the reader's
imagination; but I will not—

while yet you hold me in your arms at night,
let me betray nothing more intimate
than the roommate who blamed you for his
     cat's diseases,
or the police raid on the Moscow discotheque.

CONFESSION

Sometimes, when people are hungry,
I still want to eat; when they are naked I want to dress.

> Sometimes, even though people are homeless,
> I prefer to sleep in my own bed,

and when there's a war, I certainly don't want to fight.
Sometimes, knowing there is suffering,

> even the worst kind of oppression all over the world,
> I don't want to bear witness

or speak out or be counted or make amends.
Sometimes when you are gentle I want it rough and when
you're here

> I wish you were gone; sometimes I want him back
> and it has nothing to do with the hungry,

the naked, the homeless; sometimes it has nothing to do—
nothing whatsoever to do with you.

BUFFY RERUN POEM

It's one a.m. and I'm lying in bed,
watching a rerun of *Buffy the Vampire Slayer*,
talking to you on the phone.

I tell you Buffy is ice-skating,
and you tell me it's the episode from season two
where the assassins come to attack Buffy on the
      skating rink,

and Angel leaps onto the rink to save her,
and afterwards they kiss
and Angel pulls away in a moment of self-loathing
      and says,

I still have my vampire face on,
and Buffy touches his bumpy vampire forehead and says
I didn't even notice.

You are right, of course, about every detail—
they unfold on the muted screen at the foot of the bed
as I watch and you narrate from 200 miles away;

and Kendra appears just as you say she will,
the new slayer called up in Africa
when Buffy dies fighting the Master

in the season one finale,
and Kendra sees Angel kissing Buffy,
sees that he is a vampire and that Buffy is his girl,

so she must be evil,
and so Kendra attacks Angel at Willie's tavern,
and locks him in the cage with the transom near the ceiling,

the eastern exposure where the sunlight will soon enter
and Angel will begin to sizzle.
And I remember all these details, but only one by one,

as you recount them to me;
and I recognize the scenes, but only one by one,
as they appear before me.

But you remember it all, all the time—
you go around like that, you live your life like that,
bearing the burden of memory for us both.

YOU SEE, THE THING IS,

I've been in love before,
but never like this,
the way I lie, arm around him,
dark outside, can't sleep,
thinking of mother in a hospital bed,
lying awake while dawn comes,
yellow, gray, and slightly stale,
the hundred and eighty
degrees I turn, the away I face,
clock I check as he rolls over,
fast asleep, and catches me.

A MIDSUMMER NIGHT'S PRESS was founded by Lawrence Schimel in New Haven, CT in 1991. Using a letterpress, it published broadsides of poems by Nancy Willard, Joe Haldeman, and Jane Yolen, among others, in signed, limited editions of 126 copies, numbered 1-100 and lettered A-Z. One of the broadsides —"Will" by Jane Yolen—won a Rhysling Award. In 1993, the publisher moved to New York and the press went on hiatus until 2007, when it began publishing perfect-bound, commercially-printed books, primarily under two imprints:

FABULA RASA: devoted to works inspired by mythology, folklore, and fairy tales. Titles from this imprint include *Fairy Tales for Writers* by Lawrence Schimel, *Fortune's Lover: A Book of Tarot Poems* by Rachel Pollack, *Fairy Tales in Electri-city* by Francesca Lia Block, *The Last Selchie Child* by Jane Yolen, and *What If What's Imagined Were All True* by Roz Kaveney.

BODY LANGUAGE: devoted to texts exploring questions of gender and sexual identity. Titles from this imprint include *This is What Happened in Our Other Life* by Achy Obejas; *Banalities* by Brane Mozetic, translated from the Slovene by Elizabeta Zargi with Timothy Liu; *Handmade Love* by Julie R. Enszer; *Mute* by Raymond Luczak; *Milk and Honey: A Celebration of Jewish Lesbian Poetry* edited by Julie R. Enszer; *Dialectic of the Flesh* by Roz Kaveney; *Fortunate Light* by David Bergman; *Deleted Names* by Lawrence Schimel; and *When I Was Straight* by Julie Marie Wade.

ABOUT THE AUTHOR

MICHAEL BRODER (Freeport, New York, 1961) holds a BA in Comparative Literature from Columbia University, an MFA in Creative Writing from New York University, and a PhD in Classics from The Graduate Center of The City University of New York.

His poems, essays, and reviews have appeared in *BLOOM, Court Green, Columbia Poetry Review, Painted Bride Quarterly, Classical World,* and other journals, as well as in the anthologies *This New Breed, My Diva, Divining Divas, Rabbit Ears,* and *Ancient Obscenities.*

He has taught at Brooklyn College, Hunter College, Queens College, York College, and the Graduate Center, all of which are campuses of the City University of New York, as well as at Montclair State University (Montclair, NJ) and The University of South Carolina (Columbia, SC).

He lives in Brooklyn with his lawfully wedded spouse, the poet Jason Schneiderman, and numerous cats, both feral and domestic.

This Life Now is his first book.